D0326900

Sandgrains on a Tray

By the same author

THE RAILINGS
THE LIONS' MOUTHS

Sandgrains
on a Tray

Poems by Alan Brownjohn

MACMILLAN

© Alan Brownjohn 1969

First published 1969 by
MACMILLAN AND CO LTD
Little Essex Street London WC2
and also at Bombay Calcutta and Madras
Macmillan South Africa (Publishers) Pty Ltd Johannesburg
The Macmillan Company of Australia Pty Ltd Melbourne
The Macmillan Company of Canada Ltd Toronto
Gill and Macmillan Ltd Dublin

Printed in Great Britain by
THE BOWERING PRESS PLYMOUTH

S.D.M.W.

261168

Acknowledgements

are due to the editors of the
following, in which various of
these poems first appeared:

Allsorts 1
Ambit
The Critical Quarterly
Eight Poets
    (Poetry Book Society Pamphlet)
Encounter
The London Magazine
Micromegas
My Own Mag.
The New York Times
The North-Western Review
Outposts
Oyster
Poetry and Audience
Poetry Now
    (B.B.C. Third Programme)
The Poetry Review
Quarry
The Southern Review
The Times Literary Supplement
The Transatlantic Review
Workshop Two

A. B.

Contents

Incident on 6th August

Last and most hurting stroke of the wide,
Inescapable sunlight, a flash from some turning car's windscreen
Streaks across to my eyes and blots the whole day black.

I walk on looking out through a pulsing cloud
At the disfigured street, planting a
Seething blur on every face and dress:

They move, half-black and writhing, towards me,
Not knowing, in their late afternoon. They
Are talking and smiling and conducting their

Own concerns beneath my surface of wounds. And
Who am I to tell them they are
Scorched blotches in an insane ignorance?

They would think me the mad one.

Girl Counting

She lifts up her fawn head, nodding
Rapidly into air; she rests tensing, then
Untensing fingers on the table-top;
She closes her eyes;
And she counts, counts, with a flicker of lips breathing,
In a sort-of ecstasy of computation
—Which she gets wrong.

Such processes of icy reckoning
Seem somehow endangered by this
Devotion of her complete creatureness; by which
She renders her whole, quick, committed
Pulse to contradict all
Numeration's neat sterility:
The figures tremble as they add and rise.

And it seems all the more wrong that
We worry to put in the programming that
Conscious suffusion of some
Warmth like this, alleged to make
All the clean lights and unagitated
Dials tolerable.
While it looked only wise to bring

This human mildness in somewhere,
We should have known the struggle
Long lost before anyone ever
Began on those cool, implacable
Constructs of order and tabulation
—Clicking us into place like straight
White sticks crossed on mass graves—

And should have sensed that to
Start so late, even, was as to
Wake up that fallible, routine sentinel
To see the gulls' possible
Missile flight over his waiting screen, and
In his cavern room, to lift
His one telephone, once.

Winter Appointment

Now, after too long,
A fool's courage flows back again, and assists me
To the dentist's chair and his unheavenly lights.

The vanished space between me and this house has been
Like the gap scaring
Some anxious lover and all that he dared not risk.

Horse, hawk and debutante in the smooth magazines
Soothe, in the waiting-room, me, with tired coat and grey
Mouth. Rising, I think:

Scales of sharp justice
Appear to be carefully balancing this out:
For those gropings at pleasure, this payment of pain.

Two weeks gone since my first daring venture, when I
Knew he would not start,
And I only need fearfully submit to that

Quick, sinister, flicking parade of the wan street
Of my mouth, that tilting of searching mirrors, prods
At each drab structure,

Surveyor's verdict:
No site to be cleared, or buildings to be shored up,
Though some cleaning, for appearances, would improve.

But! —*I'll take a small X-ray of that one, in case* . . .
And two weeks of fright
Till today's visit, even if swift certainty

Soon now. (Yes . . . take a large X-ray of Diana,
I'd still not know what meant reassurance and
What shaking terror.)

*

So. Today's the day ...
Well, I *could* have shirked it ... What more helpful than to
Put off yet another painful self-attrition?

Do sit. Bleak time of revealing: no comfort here.
A train grates, roars down
The cutting outside, the smooth cat flops off the sill.

Something will have to be done ... You see there was this
Shadow like a sin I didn't think I might have
On the X-ray plate.

Nothing but to *sit*
As the cotton wool dabs at the affronted gums
And his white arm slopes to the swivel tray. But—please—

Talk, please—Rhodesia, anything—till the
Injection takes ... I'll
Lie open-mouthed at the honour of van der Byl.

A sort-of napkin fitted below my neck. 'Not
Where he eats, but where ...' (Diana-pray-grace-this-meal-
Before-and-during!)

... Christ! anything *must*
Be painful to be salutary. His foot pumps
The chair close (think of her, think of her, think of her,

Seize her presence with some poet's metaphysical
Calling of her to
This moment: for example, though he be a man

I'll allow Diana to visit the dentist:
His drill is the one of all the violations
Which purges and mends.)

Jarring suddenness;
Intermission; recommencement. *Take a good rinse.*
We are come now, I would say, to the nub of this ...

5

Pain accurately descends his cold, angled crane
Of quivering wires:
Bleak hysteria of the burr changing its note.

*

And how long do these renewals last? What hope place
In his painful skill, or in any curative
Promise I might have?

There are no answers;
Except to make a quick leap in equivocal
Relief and faith from his chair, and, to myself, say

That to have no trust in tooth mended or promise
Kept, helps no raw nerve . . .
A cavity clear, metal could firm in the space.

A sure, pure flame melted his amalgam. At last
He has carved a surface, he has stripped that napkin
Away; so I rise,

Convinced. With ball-point
I fray his dotted line, sense comfort in the gift
Of this restored street in hopeful mid-afternoon,

Down which Diana could be ready softly to
Walk, as down some now-
Cleansed and part-shuttered Piccadilly, quite alone.

Hedonist

It was not the religious pleasure-principle,
The supposed, long quest of the libertine; nor
Was it any kind of arrant desire for
Immolation in some seizing mode of brief
Forgetfulness. It was no sort of strained belief,
Or meditated act; but much more simple:

It was the sense of the sufficient good-ness
Of the next thing beyond the present thing:
The food after a day not eating,
The landing after the stairs, the prospect of some
Prospect filling the ten next minutes, should they come.
It was sleep, sometimes. But simpler even than these,

It could be just the sunlight, as an amiable event
To walk out into after the thick
Complexities of his room, leaving cigarettes, stick
And tablets and trusting, for once,
To his own feet and the friendliness of distance,
And to mere walking alone on the bright pavement.

Old Company

What is there underneath this tight and
Scarlet creasing at their eye-corners,
As the mouth-stretching laughter-spasm holds
And stacks each man's entire, shuddering
Body on top of his stomach folds?

Their faces seize in this concerted anguish.
The spread-out, cumbersome limbs around the circle
Look like helpless pain to possess.
But they will laugh, and stay. Their risen steam
Muffles each window, hides the street's greyness.

Gregarious mankind . . . Old company
Can ride down any fear as the stale
Seconds of their present unendurably tear
Them piecemeal away from those fresher
Seconds of their mutual past, where

The first laugh started. Each one's ageing face
Makes now a shield for his flesh, here where
All shields grip together grimacing
On phalanx-night against the terror
In one expressionless, unchanging thing.

Two Songs
(Homage to Louis MacNeice)

Tug out one snapping knot into flat string
                    And tie a new one
Pull out two paper-clips straight
                    And re-bend them
                    Let only your mirror weep

Cut three potatoes through
                    But hold the halves together
Break four white saucers along cracks
                    And glue the pieces
                    Let only your mirror weep

Shake out five plain clean sheets
                    And refold them
Tear six new scarves across
                    Then sew them whole
                    Let only your mirror weep

Wrench out seven firm locks
                    But fix back the jarred metals
Smash through eight wide windows
                    And cellophane the spaces
                    Let only your mirror weep

Walk a razed block round nine times
                    Aching for buildings
Refer to your death on ten occasions
                    And let the word die into silence
                    Let only your mirror weep

The pheasants rightangle away into the thicket;
The mill sails appear on the right, as the map ventures;
The sedge bends to the light wind politely, not constrained;
I love you as detail.

The church has a tower the miniature of its tower;
Finished sacks, thrown down, glitter and litter on the field;
Three day-owls scatter towards the approaching wood;
I love you for detail.

The lane turns into two ruts with a thick grass centre;
Rides of pines come thinly down to entreat at the hedge;
Hay-blocks provide for the month under polythene sheets;
I love you in detail.

Turned soil rests and waits in the damp, clean and unharried;
The concealing flat cloud glows, in foreground to the sun;
One gust flicks beads of wet from the grass at crazed angles;
I love you through detail.

Disposed to Sleep

To cry, in the near space
Between the unfolded pale screen and the bed,
Would be late, late; and would be water only.
My fluids have been less, always,
Than that impartial, other blood which now
Drips from poised foresight into
The channels under his skin.
I have not given, this or other ways.
I have, like this, gone in and out
Of bad sleep, not grasping;
Working
Dry-lip-words to half recognize
Those faces, what they came for.
                                And here the dark sister
Stands too soon by my own breathing side.

Fourth Lover

That fourth lover you mentioned, the dangerous one
Only to be talked about carefully, the one
Closest of all, still: him I will not demote too far.

I may even be generous, and allow him
One small particular duchy in
The Holy Empire of your consciousness.

Its name?—Insomniac nostalgia.

Mad Animals

In comic, unthreatening circles, the spaniel
Ran mad and fretted round the college cat;
Which sat still and just, only, looked

With at most a mild, unequivocal
Compassion. What this spaniel did was a
Sort of obsessed, yelping, bewildered

Orbit of this inexplicable creature
For a long time. It was not dignified. It was
An insanity, reproached and warned by

The gargoyles on the chapel gutter, who
Presented like frenzies, punished with
Being congealed in stone and permanent.

This was a cat of super-elegance; and
O spaniel, you to have no dignity,
Dog as you are, and self-possessed really!

What use was it to yelp? —And yet, and yet,
On an inside page in Rees-Mogg's *Times* there was,
Against all reason, news and a picture of

A cat some man had bred with spaniel's ears.

Pathetic Fallacy

Now autumn's rank enforcement of
Fawn-pointed thistle and tip-faded iris
Leaves us with this garden as an
Indifferent waste, we tend to let it alone;
We tend to light the rooms early.

We dispose to think mostly indoors, for
Outdoors only stay the limited
Tactics of inanimate things: the stray
Of blown leaves from the heap, dabs of rain
Blurring the fences, grass become irrelevant.

Nothing to think about there, we think.
Let's hug to itself the self of winter,
Glad of the close fire's flattery, happy
For winds to slam doors on us as if
It was worlds happening against our very will.

Balls of Sweetness

Before James Carra knew Anne Furlington
She made love, often, the first in both their lives,
Under a slipping mauve quilt in a seaport,
With nightlong traffic noise disturbing;
There being wallpaper the same as in her
College room; and it was Peter Daines.
It was the world. No one seemed later hurt, or
Finally betrayed.
                 It was not of consequence.

When Hester Lang told Cavan Benther that
Hidden in some long spell away from him was
A week when Philip Quernier was prepared
And it happened three times (but each time one of them
Pretended) an hour was enough for Cavan's
Fury. Nor were these people heartless. It was
Not of consequence. Such oddness at such distance
Could be healed.
                 It was the world.

Elizabeth Pender felt that past could be
Contentedly left as past concerning
William Stennett's beds where Margaret Bourn
Fought conscience and hindering fear. She
Only nodded; and thought. Such guileless frankness
Gave a lot of help. This would leave
No injury-traces . . . It was the world. In minutes
Their hands came coolly together.
                 It was not of consequence.

For my Son

Not ever to talk when merely requested,
Not ever to be the performing child,
This is what you would establish;
                              always keeping
Private and awkward counsel against
All coaxing; and going—one hopes—
The way of a good will,

To your own true designs. Which is
The way of some human institutions,
Growing not as any collective urge
                              would have them
(In its own placable image) but into
Their own more wayward value—strong,
Untidy, original, self-possessed.

Twenty-Third Day

The moon, a rejected
Gift to your disconsolate nature,
Is wasting on you its good literary

Pause in the elm branches across the river;
So that your hand leaves mine on principle, and
Complains that I make you too much the moon,
An uncomfortable ideal . . .

There is, in that, a kind of unguessed truth.
One knows, by now, the moon to be
Pock-marked, with routine mountains; thick
With feet-deep uninteresting dust
Which chokes its incursors; and worse,
She is attainable for the worst of motives.

In all, she is only a little, pale thing,
Ordinary, and human in her way (going through
Phases? You have your bloody ones; sometimes.)

—And only just staying, through inflictions
Of time and knowledge, the same, white,
Round-faced, acceptable creature.

In the Room Above

In their bed of loss they are
Like sea-things.

Her cries, like drifting gulls',
Lie ancient and somehow
Small about the air, as if wanting
Unction or pity.

A metropolis sways outside,
But in their surge of two griefs they are
Not disturbed.

—I think I know why pity comes to mind.

There was her choosing to cry,
Which she had heard was so; and there was you.

It was your silence, silence,
Made her lost and bird voice pitiful.

What we pursue pursues us,
We are such rich quarries for
Our own energies; and the long hunt hunts
Us.

Kent Archive Office, Robert Garrett:
Forebears in the Thanet Cavalry,
A squirearchic family, a ducal marriage,
Promotion aspiring to him in
Peninsular places. The fiancée's letters
Are the ladder mounting him, Imperial wars
Wage him.

He elevates money to officer-status.
How perfectly Portugal offers
Convenient insolence to be kicked downstairs!

Oh, easy it must have been, to be
Worked by instinct through wealthy alliances, to
The division in the Crimea, to
That Adjutant-Generalship . . .

Why choose this example?
It distances.
It detaches.
I am not its exact equivalent.

It's just that it's like
Any path of honourable ruin and delusion
Paving itself for the walker in pride,
Flattering his feet with challenging distances.

Pictures

Terror at night, that turns precise:
Sweat of the firebell chills my skin
With fear you lie in swathes of smoke
Too dense for rescuers to break in.

I could fling back the sheets at two,
Shake myself into waking and
Run all the roads half-clothed to where
That gaping ignorance would stand

Watching your slimness, blanket-wrapped,
Handled down ladders into the snow
As I recall those bodies were,
Was it four Boxing Nights ago?

—But then, mortality extends
To any step in any street:
There's dog-bite, or there's poison in
What small amounts of food you eat.

'Friendship is lovely'—yes, but who
Knows of all opening doors which one
Closes in velvet kindliness
And stands you facing someone's gun?

This way, the horrors flock around,
The fears come pestering. —And yet
Their idiot multiplicity
Provides a kind of safety-net:

If I decide sometimes to dread
Your falling down on every stair,
Just as irrationally I could
Think you strode safely anywhere.

If death could wait on any step,
Conversely you might stay intact
From any earthly wound or stain
Your sort-of innocence might attract.

And leaving every profitless
Anxiety which coats the breath:
There is one fantasy I feel
A *little* likelier than death:

A day in sultry weather, soon,
To sit and think, idly, to where
Some momentary fatigue has bent
Your shoulders . . . With a casual air

You stretch; and all that row of beads
Rides upwards on your stretching dress
—My fingers stretch out miles to touch
Their spacing red-and-yellowness.

Would this aspiring gesture set
Some small telepathy in train?
Encouraged by the thought, I go
And try the telephone, again.

—Anna's voice. You are called. Downstairs
You answer with far-off surprise,
Slow, as you yawn and curse, to see
Anything with your naked eyes.

You take your glasses from the shelf,
Hold, and unfold, them, to the light,
Flick them across your sleeve, and put
Them on, so that your world seems right,

—And speak. Although you often hate
Suggestions made when you are tired,
This time some sixth and lucky sense
Tells you what answer is required.

Distance can cancel out itself,
But slowly! Thought is faster than
Speeds at which engines or mere feet
Can move to carry any man.

But finally your street, too warm
Under that gathering summer cloud,
Arrives. And when the intercom
Takes up your syllable aloud,

The lock releases. As my steps
Run to the inner door upstairs,
You stack some records on, and make
To rearrange the couch and chairs . . .

Some time earlier in the week,
We cleaned this room. These cushions take
A gentler attitude, one feels,
For every kind and prescient shake.

The window's wide. You jump to see
Your curtains snatched into the storm,
But something lucky I think to say
Makes laughter of your half-alarm.

The Indian shade veiling the lamp
Clicks, in the draught which shuts the door.
Anna is out. The phone is dead.
You nudge four shoes towards the floor.

Braceleted and bare, your arm
Stretches to drop on a low shelf
Your folded glasses. How the rain slants.
Gently the record plays itself.

That table-lamp again. It has
Horsemen mounting a fawn hill.
The edge of its hushed arc of light
Quivers; and yet the draught is still.

There are some fish that drift about
And at each breathing close their eyes,
As if replenishments of air
Came each on each a sweet surprise . . .

No matter . . . Half-an-hour in one track
—A kind of blues, but sweet enough—
The automatic pick-up arm
Achieves its end and switches off.

Much social detail you don't need.
Fuller descriptions of the flat?
Or names, or times, or what we drank?
Invent your own. And leave it that

As well as pictures in each eye
We get slipped discs and are let lie
In some large, liberal, hospital
Bed together, so that all

The learned doctors might come near
(Oh, not to diagnose, but) to hear
Wild, whimsical, allusive range
Of talk, on questions rich and strange

For, laid on boards to straighten us
For all things curved and tortuous,
Day upon day we languish there
And talk, from Twardzik to Voltaire.

Breaking Eggs

It is as if she chose to exist
To scathe forgivable sins
—In which she could be right;

But to watch her way, for example,
With pardonable pride, or any faintly
False dignity or ceremoniousness

Is somehow terrible.
                And to prepare a meal
(Though no one should dare to asperse her skill),
She will unclasp each poised, mature

Vegetable's grip upon itself, leaf
By pathetic leaf, intently; or crack
The fragile and decorous eggs

With rapid and curt fingers, not smiling.
It would look like no more than cold spite
If it were not her own kind of care; and

If she could not also, with a mere knife only,
Take up (precise and chilling miracle!)
Each omelette into surging fabric-folds.

Seven Activities for a Young Child

Turn on the tap for straight and silver water in the sink,
Cross your finger through
The sleek thread falling
                    —*One.*

Spread white sandgrains on a tray,
And make clean furrows with a bent stick
To stare for a meaning
                    —*Two.*

Draw some clumsy birds on yellow paper,
Confronting each other and as if to fly
Over your scribbled hill
                    —*Three.*

Cut rapid holes into folded paper, look
At the unfolded pattern, look
Through the unfolded pattern
                    —*Four.*

Walk on any square stone of the pavement,
Or on any crack between, as long
As it's with no one or with someone
                    —*Five.*

Throw up a ball to touch the truest brick
Of the red-brick wall,
Catch it with neat, cupped hand
                    —*Six.*

Make up in your head a path, and name it,
Name where it will lead you,
Walk towards where it will lead you
                    —*Seven.*

One, two, three, four, five, six, seven:
Take-up-the-rag-doll-quietly-and-sing-her-to-sleep.

This coarse road, my road, struggles out
South-east across London, an exhausted
Grey zigzag of stubborn, unassimilable
    Macadam, passing hoardings pasted

With blow-ups of cricket journalists, blackened
And not-quite-Georgian terraces,
Shagged-out Greens of geraniums and
    Floral coats-of-arms, lost pieces

Of genteel façade behind and above
Lyons' shopfronts and 'Pullum Promotions',
—Journeying between wired-off bombed lots glossy
    With parked Consuls, making diversions

Round bus depots and draggled estates
In circumlocutory One-Ways,
Netting aquaria in crammed pet store windows,
    Skirting multi-racial bingo queues,

And acquiring, for its self-hating hoard, old black-railed
Underground bogs advising the Seamen's Hospital,
'Do-it-yourself' shops, 'Funerals and Monuments', and
    Victorian Charrington pubs. All

Along its length it despoils, in turn, a sequence
Of echoless names: Camberwell, Peckham,
New Cross Gate; places having no recorded past
    Except in histories of the tram.

It takes out, in cars, arterial affluence
At week-ends, returning it as bad blood
To Monday mornings in town. It is altogether
    Like a vein travelled by hardy diseases, an aged

Canal dredgeable for bodies left behind
On its soulless travels: Sixty-Nine,
Thirty-Six, One-Eight-Five. It takes no clear
    Attitude anyone could easily define

So as to resist or admire it. It seems to hate you
Possessively, want to envelop you in nothing
Distinguishable or distinguished, like its own
    Smothered slopes and rotting

Valleys. This road, generally, is one for
The long-defeated; and turns any ironic
Observer's tracer-isotope of ecology,
    Sociology, or hopeful manic

Verse into a kind of mere
Nosing virus itself. It leaves its despondent, foul
And intractable deposit on its own
    Banks all the way like virtually all

Large rivers, particularly the holy ones, which it
Is not. It sees little that deserves to be undespised.
It only means well in the worst of ways.
    How much of love is much less compromised?

The Clouds

The craftsmen in my line bred out.
I drive, but could I mend a fuse.
My fathers handled founts of words
My brain would catch and fingers lose.

I find a fair excuse, to serve:
There has, in our society,
Been 'social change', which makes these skills
Much less of a necessity.

Beyond your shoulder I can see
A saucer—stamped out by machine—
On the formica shelf near where
We lie on quilts of terylene.

No sort of ancient expertise
Goes to create these modern things:
To them, no craftsman's hand its pride
Or love for their completeness brings.

Their very make and feel rejects
Any thought that such loving powers
Nurtured their shapes to what they are
Through someone's calm and patient hours.

That care seems obsolete.—Yes, I know
You were your parents' artefact,
Your perfect head, shoulders and back
Made in a sort-of skilful act,

But when I move a care-ful hand
(No craftsman's art its legacy)
And dot a pattering line to count
Your poised and tensing vertebrae,

It's not *great* numeracy I want,
Or flair for cold technologies
—Such details are not wanted in
All kinds of loving enterprise.

Nor do we need such skills to lose
All sense of this room, house and street . . .
And don't doubt, though we use no craft,
That love it is makes this complete.

—And, well, on looking up I see,
As a sweet end to summer's drought,
Some wholly unskilled clouds which pour
Blessings of rain on Baron's Court.

Cars
(A Variation on Andrey Vosnesensky : 'Bikes')

the switching off and the final shake into
silence is a bold instant: to have exposed,
even at night and in a strange district,
your number and your face to all

those possible eyes! it took
a moment's real bravery.
                         but after the next
day undiscovered, and then through
gradually the weeks after, it became

marvellously easy to have done. the heavy
detritus of schemes and breakdowns, all that
weight of mistaken journeys, all
the money and sweat finished, well, a relief!

and the council can't find labour to drag it
away, not them. it joins the one in the next
street and the one in the street after in a vast
network of abandonment.

it looks through its windscreen at the trees of the
scraggy suburb as they grow; and responds to wary
curiosity with certainty at last. unseen, the
scavengers come back for item after item.

we'll forgive and pity them, with a sort-of patronage,
the termites who swarm over tyres, flashers, tappets,
by day or by night and pocket them to fit up
their own structures of temporary hopefulness.

Fortune

Whirling through January, a conclave
Of echoes under a parapet, sleet furring the sheep, and
A cord of salt unthreading onto the table:
      A yellow bell, an orange, a yellow bell.

Circling round April, a syllable scratched in ash,
And flicking past arches on a motorway, though
A white cat waited and washed at the downstairs door:
      A yellow bell, a yellow bell, a peach.

Turning through August, the complexions of two
Terrains various as Iceland and Rumania,
Then that important ladder she walked beneath:
      A grapefruit, a yellow bell, a yellow bell.

Spinning in December, and snow spinning, and her
Feet drawn in close on a tall chair, when
Somehow the mirror fled her superstitious hand
      —Three lots of grapes in mauve, ironical clusters!

To Sleep; on St Lucy's Day

Shadow containing all shades, glad
Enemy or eluding lover, rabidly
Changeable and sly one, here then
Is the shortest day's tribute, made
In merging, unaccountable images:
Chestnuts fallen on the random
Grass at Hales where the blood once
Lipped the barbaric phial; crude
Skull-bone under a woman's eyes unable
To hide or feign; men wounding
Sweet animals and weeping; music
Becoming phrases becoming music.

                                  Who
Could hold and follow these back to
Say the loose paving stone in the adult
Street this morning, where it
Tripped the crying child? Shadow,
They are yours to understand, and
To repeat; wilted
Wreaths in nightly giving.

                              Where
Gods are most firm and ancient, you
Are new always, and never certain;
Youthful; a slow, calm hand, or a face
Followed and escaping. Those whom
You love hardly need to dispose limbs,
Or resolve on blankness to invoke you,
But wait merely, only a short time.
Those you despise,
Their bodies char and live in sullen
Fires of wakefulness, quartering and
Rejoining at each chime. Between, lie
All your various supplicants, meditative
Or sad-uneasy, sensing
—So many hundred ways—their

Thoughts meet, link, dissolve into
Illogic, leave consciousness.
                    Why
Are you, in whole Valhallas of
Straight gaze and iron purposings,
Most sickly and inconstant, working your power
Through unexpectedness (we never
See you, but only, ever, wake
To know that you have passed)?
You stay invisible; and yet, last night,
Ruining and re-begetting, you
Came without terror or long delay,
Your footfall unhurried, your words
Kindly and sure, telling no lie, and
Your arms folding round without
An ambiguous glance, and you were clear and
Quick, as petals quivering in daylight.

Somehow

The North Lancashire Ballet Group is coming
Next month, and Miriam Granger-White is giving
A Francis Thompson reading in the Public
Library. So we are all well catered for, culture-wise,
And don't really miss London. It's interesting
How many talented people do in fact
Choose the provinces: you seem to get
Room to breathe here somehow, and so many

Advantages (for instance, the post for London
Goes as late as *eleven* on weekdays!). We have these
Musician friends—the husband's often having things
Done by the choir of Radio Chesterfield, the wife
Lectures in a College of Education—they're like us,
They gave up London because it just didn't seem
To offer the scope somehow. Robert's work is
Going awfully well; as I think I told you, it's

An open-minded, progressive sort of firm, and he has
The chance to do a small, quite modern, country
Cottage for a retired solicitor. He's pretty sure
The standard is as high as a lot of firms
In London. I do several hours each week
Helping at the Family Planning Clinic, there's plenty
To occupy us. Yes, we keep in touch, we can
Get most of our old friends on S.T.D.,

And people really do exaggerate about the northern
Weather. I wouldn't at all like to have
To drive the Anglia in London traffic. I don't think
I could. There's a design shop in the Market Square
Where you can get almost anything, a delicatessen
With every kind of bread we like, and
A fabric shop as good as Oxford Street. Robert
Is on the Third Programme Listeners' Panel.

We are growing lobelias for the local Help the Depressives
Flower Show, which keeps us busy. It's
A good life. Would you like to come down?
We have an enormous spare room and it would
Be lovely to see you. You could stay as long as
You like—we wouldn't bother you. It's
Quite possible, don't you think, to be 'provincial'
While actually living in the metropolis? Anyway,

Write soon, tell us your news, love to Amanda.

Found under Capricorn

disappointments   showdowns   odd acquaintances?
no   you can expect   happy circumstances
compliments   good things   calm   finances

planetary influences   say something   of ambition
think constructively   change of climate or infection
shouldn't bother you   but   plan   any   situation

let your enthusiasm carry you   deal with   business
like   new moon   plans   celebrate   friendliness
among   times of   deep happiness

everything should steadily improve   gradually
the world   spring   life   your sheer   property
the sun is passing through   exciting   harmony

Common Sense

An agricultural labourer, who has
A wife and four children, receives 20s a week.
¾ buys food, and the members of the family
Have three meals a day.
How much is that per person per meal?
—*From Pitman's Common Sense Arithmetic, 1917*

A gardener, paid 24s a week, is
Fined 1/3 if he comes to work late.
At the end of 26 weeks, he receives
£30. 5. 3. How
Often was he late?
—*From Pitman's Common Sense Arithmetic, 1917*

A milk dealer buys milk at 3d a quart. He
Dilutes it with 3% water and sells
124 gallons of the mixture at
4d per quart. How much of his profit is made by
Adulterating the milk?
—*From Pitman's Common Sense Arithmetic, 1917*

The table printed below gives the number
Of paupers in the United Kingdom, and
The total cost of poor relief.
Find the average number
Of paupers per ten thousand people.
—*From Pitman's Common Sense Arithmetic, 1917*

An army had to march to the relief of
A besieged town, 500 miles away, which
Had telegraphed that it could hold out for 18 days.
The army made forced marches at the rate of 18
Miles a day. Would it be there in time?
—*From Pitman's Common Sense Arithmetic, 1917*

Out of an army of 28,000 men,
15% were
Killed, 25% were
Wounded. Calculate
How many men there were left to fight.
>   —*From Pitman's Common Sense Arithmetic, 1917*

These sums are offered to
That host of young people in our Elementary Schools, who
Are so ardently desirous of setting
Foot upon the first rung of the
Educational ladder ...
>   —*From Pitman's Common Sense Arithmetic, 1917*

Taking Amanda back to St Winefride's

As I drove,
to see what
came I was
looking in
the driving
mirror and
saw Aman-
da's face glazed
at air, at
some turn of
the talk. This
was danger . . .
Switch the talk
to something
else, quickly,
please.
        It switched.
We ran up
between two
hedges of
spurting flowers,
the soft clouds
flocked above
to the sun,
quite a fine
afternoon.
I smoked.
        Three
people in
this car in
a country
trip to a
—a house: so
obvious,
easy and

Amanda's
eyes clear now.
Yet I still
saw it there,
another
closing face
seen elsewhere,
with its own
purposed kind
of rigid
calm, and blank
light; and guessed
the intent
look it had
was someone's

very mad.

Comforts

The precisions of idleness:
A ball hit through a hoop on a lawn,
The table-top grained and bare, to which
You take a thin, scrawling pen and paper.
Also, rain is at the green window, scratching.

—Or, posing a record, leaving it
To settle itself, to play;
Or, an immovability about certain white cards
In a shelf-row . . .
Such things, therefore. And, I dare
You, I dare you, disorder.

Flat Place

There is a prevailing power about certain flat lands:
A sort-of tenacity of fens, draining
The strength of the eye away upon
Glamourless perspectives.

What asks no effort over any
Rising, exciting slope, offers the same way no
Ease of declension through soft, hushed
Valleys . . . Consequently,
Nothing there climaxes very much, or
Falls back spent, either.

And the least landmarks—windmills,
Meagre churches, pebble-heaps—practise
Only a small, ironic punctuation, not a
Sudden significance; resembling in this
The comments of a woman watching
Her own ravishment fail, as
She suffers it passively, keeping herself
Virgin with an amused detachment.

A Progress

The slipping tile,
The broken stile across the path,
And a clatter of scaring tinsel over
Cropless fields.

Yes, well, if I were you I would
Take a different walk today:
Get on some steady stretch, and
Forget such funerary crusts.

And yet I would somehow prefer
To extend the same kind of walk and muster
Every next image of worry, if I could,
Into a sense of power.

Surely ... yet we are all measured by
How much, and with what grace and humour we
Tug those hands anti-clockwise, wanting to try
To fix a time not late enough to die.

Peter Daines at a Party

Oliver Cromwell and Beethoven both
Died in the middle of thunderstorms. Ruth
Didn't know this, but knew Kierkegaard's Dad
Cursed God from a hilltop, or so it was said.
Yet none of these things was at all familiar
To Mary, or Nora, or Helen, or Pamela.

But Pamela knew of some laws of Justinian's,
Helen listened to Schutz and had read *The Virginians*,
And Nora and Mary liked Wallace Stevens,
So in general terms it worked out evens
—Except that none of them, only Amanda,
Knew that Oliver Cromwell had died during thunder.

Still, here were these women with items of knowledge
Picked up in one and another college
—And here am I with not quite all their gaps
In my knowledge of all these high-powered chaps,
Doing well with the female population
And their limited but charming conversation.

Sestina in Memoriam Vernon Watkins

When, that October, he was at Attingham, I first
Saw him in the early evening: treading with a good
Relaxed stride down the kitchen garden, only to then
Pause under a little brick archway and wonder
If there were really time for a walk before supper, and at last
Turn back, avoiding the rain, to the great

House, to unpack instead.
     Out of a great
Metal trunk lashed up with ropes, he took first
His poems and notes, then some very orderly clothes, and, at the
 last
Moment, nearly missing the meal, needing to be a 'good
Listener', on the stairs, to a lady full of wonder
At the naturalness of a famous poet, he ate his roast beef, then

Signed a few copies of *Affinities* over coffee, then
Told precise, nostalgic anecdotes of the last
Time he encountered Dylan Thomas; stopping to wonder
How it was he never somehow got beyond the first
Shots at teaching him to drive, on Pendine Sands.
       Though good
For several more hours' talk, we did at last

Wander off in search of our respective rooms, the last
People to go to bed; but not knowing where we were, then
Had to grope our way, lost, through innumerable great
State-rooms of irreplaceable relics, probably a good
Half-mile from the room where we first
Sat—and were finally caught up by the Warden, starting to
 wonder

Who it was prowling about . . . I do wonder
Why, when most men drop *two* shoes on the floor above, the last
I heard of Vernon Watkins that night was his dropping first

45

One, then a second, then a *third* . . . It must have then
Been well past two . . . But he was up early working on a great
Pile of other people's verses, which he covered with neat good

Advice; and at eleven gave his Yeats memorial poem, a good
One to finish with, a fine bardic rendering, from a lectern. I
    wonder,
Still, how his taxi got him to the station in time: it could be, great
And mysterious assistance saved him, in this last
Frantic departure . . .
                   Still . . .
                         Mere irrelevant scraps? But then
He had this sort-of quality—no one's first

Virtue, and not *his* first, but one power his good-ness had,
Then as always: to give all quirks and details a sort of odd
    wonder,
Each last, least, great thing asking wry gratitudes.

Man Watching

Is it the horse explains the field,
Which he exists to crop; or that the field

Is only grown at all to make
The horse's nourishment?
                              Whichever way,

The two can yield, at dawn, an
Aesthetic incident: slight mist,

The slow grass growing, the slow
Horse turning; and the man

Watching as he stands in the first sun
On the revolving earth.

Lines for a Birthday

Born fourth out of five. Mother
Had maxims about sunrise and godly
Demeanours. Father went
Away and it wasn't allowed to . . . She
Made him a 'very famous
Scientist'. Fostered, on various
Homes of indigent Florida,
Calling from the table, 'I'm
Starving!' Swam early. Told
Sister at ten, 'If you let the bath-water
Run on you *there*, it gets
Like you kind-of can't *bear* it . . .'
And lay with her, nights, pretending
It was Elvis. Went to High
School, was once voted
Student 'most likely to succeed'
In the year. Collected a
Pack of girls for constructive
Depravity, sat on a long bonnet
For a boy's camera, proposed
Club colours black and grey, was
Fired and let other leaders
Mess it up latterly. Cheered, danced,
Wrote the club song and found
How all the boys tried making it on
Peppermint tongues and false, sun-
Hot leather in coupés. Ran
From the house when sister could
Nearly have been dying; and blamed
Herself. Looked a long time with
Brother, for a Coleridge, to
Complete themselves. Lost It
In five jerks of a quarterback's
Ass . . . homo ludens . . . he hasn't ever
Married. Saved up for U.C.L.A., nearly

A Republican; Civil Rights
At Berkeley. Stayed Karl's
Flat in the poor quarter—and
Went to Mexico for the first one
(Corner of the avenue: 'Americano?'
'Si!' Christ lifted her away
Through the pentothal). Good grades,
Naturally, and surfed on the beaches;
Broke down about obsessions with
Filling, every, single, moment . . . met
With Joe Missile, that being
The second time: a phone call to the flat. 'Say,
Did you get your . . . ?' 'No.' Done in
San Diego. Crying in a
Waiting room, yet bored by
Comforting in only six weeks,
Went six
Thousand miles, married, carried
Her mother's admonitions. Adopted
Cats, put down a mortgage, was
Pursued across rooms with knives.
Ate and ate and spoke about it,
Invented William and Rosemary, covers
For lovers. Recalled how
Last summer started working the
Harmless fantasies: Greeks, Finns,
Admirers, haters, blackmailers, mechanics,
Lecturers; had thought to let in
Some of all the professions that . . .
Left, for her own flat; found
The tap in the *centre* of the bathroom wall,
Had 'waited all my life for such a tap—but
The water was ice-cold!'
Taught some people, wrote an exercise,
Lived in a station, lay with this
Frenchman, Saturday, above
Knightsbridge. Today
Cut her forearms in unimportant
Places over the sink, writes, 'Leave

Me, forgive me, this
Is the tomorrow I have chosen, the
Suicide it will mean.' And now the white
Sun rises as we drive south, with
The power-station ambiguously
Applauding, and
Tomorrow is happy
Birthday, Lauren, happy
Birthday, Lauren, happy
Birthday.

Ballad for a Birthday

I cleaned up the house, and moved the telephone;
I had a look to see if the plant had grown;
I put Tiddles outside, and sat on my own:
      I feel the same, but I wouldn't want to call it love.

I arranged my dresses on laundry hooks;
I pulled out the table and set out my books;
I went to the window for just one or two looks:
      I feel the same, but I wouldn't want to call it love.

I wanted coffee, so I marked the page;
It should have been over when it got to this stage;
Can I *be* the same girl at a different age?
      I feel the same, but I wouldn't want to call it love.

What if he phoned, and I heard the bell
With my feet on the bath-tap, and I couldn't tell . . .
Well, I heard it . . . should I answer it as well?
      I feel the same, but I wouldn't want to call it love.

If he wrote a letter, saying Could we meet,
Or if we met by accident, in the street
—When something's finished, is it *always* complete?
      I feel the same, but I wouldn't want to call it love.

If he drove round here and knocked on the door,
Would I answer his questions, let him ask me more,
Or could I tell him I was absolutely sure . . . ?
      —Oh, I feel the same, but I wouldn't want to *call* it love.

In the Visitors' Book

Straight north across Norfolk, the lanes
Lead on past shrines and staithes to assuage
All thirst for greenness and lucidity,
And present at last the Meals and Bights of
An exhausted, exalted coast.
                                        And there start
The contradictions. The spring tide in April is
No resurrection of crested energies, but
A cagey, persistent ripple towards us
Under ghost sunlight, quietly
Marooning the yellowed freshes. Boards
Painted with warnings compromise the apparent
Calm of a sea you could walk into
For placid furlongs. It doesn't feel right, but
Here there seems nothing in the world except
Paradox, any more; and to
Wake after afternoon sleep is a
Reincarnation to the inconsistency of
One's existing at all with this archaic flesh,
Combining, like this place, such aged
And such fervent weathers.
                                        Inland,
The mills casually circle, the cattle
Diffuse in an amiable way over
Ample and undulant clovers, and
The land is quite logically patterned
And fruitful. The silences there
Add layer on layer to themselves, in
Immense stage pauses; disquieting, but
A less ambiguous peace than the sky's
White wideness here over these ancient,
Incredible sandgrains.
                                        There is nothing on
This coast at all comfortable: even inconse-
Quential things are ominous with a hint

Of the not-to-be-explained: little metal
Grids in the water, abandoned
Clothes in the dunes, a quick wheeling-
Off of birds for no detectable
Reason.
        And unless you love them, this
Many antitheses would amount in an hour
To a request to go elsewhere; which
We, at least, did not obey until,
Rising from the reed-cries of love we saw
Five black undrowned sisters of chastity
Receding in the very naked light along
The foam-line, with footsteps arrogantly
Murdering the assoiled sand.
                It was
Tribute of a further contradiction, almost
Deserving what we had just quite freely
Taken: the freedom of the place.

Notes on Some of the Poems

A member of the audience at a poetry reading asked why, if I gave explanatory comments before reading certain poems, notes should not be added when the poems appeared in a volume. Some explanation, helpful when people are hearing a poem for the first time, is of course unnecessary when they have time to consider it more slowly on the page. But possibly certain indications from the writer will serve to provoke a dialogue between the reader and the poem. These notes should be taken that way, not as attempts to extenuate the poems or patronise the reader and do his work for him.

Incident on 6th August: the date is Hiroshima Day. One or two readers who ventured to be interested by the poem have felt trapped into a sort-of protest posture when this was made clear.

Winter Appointment: the psychological significance of extreme fear of the dentist has been confidentially pointed out to me. Mr van der Byl was Deputy Minister of Information in Mr Ian Smith's cabinet when the poem was written: perhaps *some* deference to the politics of a dentist when one is in his chair is not too much of a compromise. Comparing a mouth of healthy, filled teeth to a shuttered Piccadilly (at the end of the poem) is possibly a bit Clevelandesque and puritanical.

Old Company suggested itself in the midst of the bluff pathos of an Old Boys' Dinner.

Disposed to Sleep: the title and the situation are in *2 Henry IV*, iv. v.

Mad Animals: the original cat and spaniel, which, much later, provided the metaphor for a human predicament, were the college cat of Merton College, Oxford, and the dog of the late Professor H. W. Garrod. The cat with spaniel ears, bred by Mr William Ross of Clackmannan, was in *The Times* of 9th March 1967.

KAO U888: Mr Donald Gibson writes about General Garrett in *Archaeologia Cantiana*, vol. lxxxi (1966). The General's documents are shelved at *U888* in the Kent Archive Office. Careerists, even when successful and happy, often seem somehow victimised by their own energies in the eyes of onlookers.

Pictures: the pictures are ambitious daydreams, but the word recalled Donne's 'And pictures in our eyes to get/Was all our propagation' ('The Ecstasy'). The jazz pianist Richard Twardzik (last line) died in 1955 at 24; and only half of an LP perpetuates the work of this brilliant performer.

Cars: Vosnesensky's bicycles are romantic and evocative, yet more energetic than the western equivalent: abandoned cars.

Fortune: a woman is playing a fruit machine.

Somehow satirises not the provinces but a certain provincial habit of mind.

Found under Capricorn: horoscope columns in women's magazines don't provide uninterrupted poetic diction, so there are gaps between the extracts. Perhaps this is, like *Common Sense*, a 'collage', rather than a 'found' poem.

Sestina in Memoriam Vernon Watkins: gravity seemed to me not always necessary for a memorial poem; and it was, anyway, a lively and memorably stimulating week-end because of one whom it is very difficult to imagine no longer with us. Attingham Park is the adult education centre near Shrewsbury.

DATE DUE